W9-AXK-643

ANIMAL SCAVENGERS

Army Ants

SANDRA MARKLE

LERNER PUBLICATIONS COMPANY / MINNEAPOLIS

The Animal World is Full of SCAVENGERS.

Scavengers are the cleanup crew who find and eat carrion (dead animals) in order to survive. Every day, animals are born and animals die. Without scavengers, the bodies of dead animals would rot away slowly. The decaying flesh would smell bad and take up space. It could also pollute water and attract flies and other disease-carrying insects. Fortunately, scavengers everywhere eat dead and dying animals before they have time to rot. In the tropical parts of Africa, South America, Central America, and Asia, army ants often work together to kill weak, sick, and old animals, as well as eating dead creatures. *Many millions of army ants are part of the tropical forest cleanup crew.*

There are more than three hundred different kinds of army ants in the world. Most spend their entire lives underground and are never seen. But some kinds of army ants search for food on the surface. Two of these are *Dorylus,* or driver ants, which live in Africa, and these *Eciton* ants, which live in South and Central America. Like many army ant colonies, this one is huge! As many as twenty million ants may be living together.

Army ant colonies are made up mainly of female ants. Males aren't made until they're needed to mate with the colony's single fertile female, the queen. She produces all of the colony's offspring. Queen ants, like this one, are the largest members of the colony and may be as big as an adult human's thumb.

The colony has millions of female worker ants like these. They're not able to lay eggs, but they do all the other jobs in the colony.

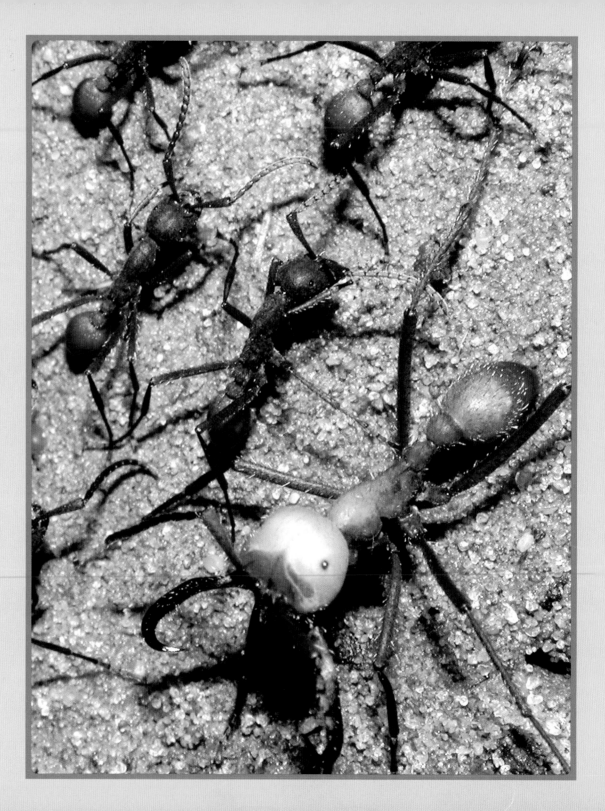

For example, the biggest *Eciton* and *Dorylus* worker ants have extra large mandibles, or toothlike mouthparts. These are perfect biting weapons. The workers use them to defend the colony against beetles, lizards, birds, and other predators that might attack or try to steal food. For this reason, the largest army ant workers are often called soldiers or majors.

Soldiers, with their big mandibles, can't grip and carry anything. Slightly smaller, or submajor, army ant workers have smaller mandibles that are just right for gripping. These ants are porters, carrying food back to the nest. The nest is the place where the queen and the brood (developing young) stay. Submajors also have extra long legs to help them carry the food beneath their bodies.

The smallest, or minor, workers stay at the nest and help the queen and the brood. The minor workers carry the eggs the queen lays to a place where they can hatch. The workers also feed the growing young, called larvae. The minors carry the eggs and larvae when the colony moves. Minor workers haul leftover bits of food and any dead workers to the colony's garbage dump.

It's early morning and the Costa Rican rain forest in Central America is dripping from a rain shower. As the forest heats up, the *Eciton* army ants warm up too and become more active. Soon they are on the move. The nearly one million workers create a noisy rustling as their tiny feet strike the leaf litter on the forest floor. Because the ants eat flesh, a strong odor of spoiled meat hangs over them. Suddenly, the leaf litter appears to boil as cockroaches, centipedes, spiders, and other creatures flee the approaching swarm.

Ants called pioneers run ahead of the others along the front of the swarm. As each of these ants doubles back, it drags its tail end. Each pioneer secretes a bit of pheromone, a checmical scent, from its tail to mark a new trail. Other ants follow this trail. Then the pioneers in this group run back to the swarm, strengthening the trail for still others to follow.

Eciton workers are nearly blind. Their world is mostly shaped by the feel of the surfaces they touch and the chemicals they detect with their feet and antennae.

As the trail gets stronger, more ants follow. Soon a solid mass of ants more than 30 feet (about 10 meters) wide is following the trail.

The pioneering workers reach a hole in the leaf litter that is too wide to cross easily. Then the front workers stretch out their legs. Other ants climb onto their sisters, anchor themselves with their claw-tipped feet, and stretch out too. Ant by ant, chains of workers build up. Some of the ants in these chains reach out to hook up with ants on either side of them. This way the ants become a living bridge that the other members of the colony can cross. Then the army moves on, traveling as fast as 65 feet (20 m) per hour.

Suddenly, the army encounters an injured scorpion that only barely survived a fight for a mate. The submajor workers immediately attack, stinging the scorpion. As the army ants climb all over the dark-bodied scorpion, they sting it, injecting venom (a liquid poison). The scorpion dies quickly. Once the scorpion stops moving, the workers grip it and pull. The venom has dissolved the soft tissue that holds together the hard parts of the scorpion's body. The ants are able to pull it to bits.

One porter ant climbs onto the scorpion's tail, bites to hold on, and starts running. By carrying the scorpion's weight under its body, the worker can handle a heavy load. But the scorpion's tail is so big that this single ant can't go very fast. Another worker grabs onto the load too and runs along with the first worker.

Meanwhile, a pioneer worker senses the odor of a praying mantis. She goes in that direction. When she returns to the swarm, she dashes to the left and to the right, touching her sister workers with her antennae. This tells them to join her. Some follow immediately, while others dash off to recruit more workers before following the pioneer's trail. Within seconds, thousands of workers are swarming over the praying mantis. Then they sting and tear it into bits and start hauling this food home too.

Soon there's a traffic jam between ants coming and going away from the nest to find food. Two sister workers going in opposite directions bump into each other. The ant carrying a load moves forward in a straight line. The other ant veers to one side. This creates a center nest-bound lane between the two outbound swarms of ants. Alongside the ant's highway system, the soldiers form an advancing line to guard the traveling workers.

Soldier ants protect their colony from insect enemies. Whenever a soldier ant senses something besides a member of its colony, the soldier rears up on its hind end. It opens its large mandibles wide to attack. This threat often turns away silverfish, beetles, flies, and other predators of ants.

Meanwhile, the other workers head home with their food bits. They don't eat any of the food as they carry it back to the nest.

Back at the nest, the workers tear apart any solid chunks of food they carried. As they do this, they eat the juice that's squeezed out of the food chunk. This juice goes into their crop, a storage sack in their digestive system. The crop holds the food before it passes into the stomach. Workers share some of this stored food juice with the workers in the nest one drop at a time. The nest workers roll the soft bits of food into pellets and drop this food onto the larvae to feed them. Or they may carry the larvae onto a pile of the food pellets.

From dawn until dusk, the workers forage (hunt for food) and carry food home. Then, as the light in the forest dims and the air cools, the traffic flow within the swarm changes. The returning workers run into a swarm of workers leaving the nest site. The colony has eaten all of the nearby food. It is moving to a new area where there is a fresh food supply. The workers will begin to collect food in the new area the next day.

The returning workers join the ants leaving the nest. They carry the colony's eggs and developing young along with them. Eventually, the queen goes too, surrounded by her attending group of worker ants.

The army ant colony may travel as little as 6 feet (2 m) or more than 300 feet (91 m) during the night before it picks a nest site. *Dorylus* ants always nest underground. Surface-living *Eciton* ants settle in above ground, temporary nests while they are traveling. When the *Eciton* workers come to a fallen tree, some hook their claw-tipped feet to the wood and hang over the edge. Then others climb down these workers, hook on and stretch out, forming a living chain of ants.

Soon a number of these ant chains hook together, creating a living curtain that protects the nest site under the fallen tree. Behind the curtain of ant bodies, more workers surround the brood. They also surround the queen, who is near the center of the brood. It rains during the night, but the bodies of the ants forming the living curtain shed the water, and the rest of the colony stays dry.

Like all ants, army ants go through three stages as they develop into adults—egg, larva, and pupa. The queen lays the eggs that hatch into the larvae. The larvae eat the food pellets prepared by the workers and grow bigger. Then the larvae become pupae, a stage in which the developing young doesn't eat or move.

When the larvae develop into pupae, the *Eciton* colony moves into an underground cavity. This will be the colony's nest for about two weeks. Inside the pupae cases, the young change into their adult form before they emerge again. These adults will become the work force that finds food for the next brood hatching from the eggs the queen lays.

Meanwhile, the queen's abdomen has been swelling. She's preparing to lay another big brood. The queen starts laying eggs by the second week the colony is in its underground nest site. The minor workers carry the eggs to nest chambers where they will hatch into larvae. Most of the eggs the queen lays become larvae that will develop into workers. But this time, the queen also lays eggs that hatch into larvae that will become males and new queens.

Unlike other members of the colony, adult male *Eciton* have wings and eyes that can see well. They need to be able to fly and see because they will leave their birth colony to go in search of a mate.

When the new queens and males emerge from the pupa stage, the colony splits in half. Two swarms, instead of one, are sent out. They travel in opposite directions. Eventually, each swarm begins to form a nest. Then the old queen competes with the new queens in a race to be the first to arrive at one of the new nests. The race is over when each new colony has a queen.

Meanwhile, the male *Eciton* ants fly out in search of other *Eciton* colonies. Some fail. A hungry spider caught this male army ant.

If a male does find a colony, he joins a swarm of foraging workers. At this point, he loses his wings naturally or the workers pull them off. Then they either kill him or they let him move through the swarm to mate with their queen.

During mating, the male deposits cells called sperm with the queen. Then, shortly afterward, he dies. The queen stores the sperm she received in a sack inside her body. Each egg she produces will merge with a sperm in order for a larva to start developing. But because the queen can store a lot of sperm and hold it for long periods, she can produce a huge number of young before she needs to mate again.

So even as some members of the colony die, plenty of new workers are produced to replace them. The cycle of life and foraging for food in the forest continues. And the army ant colony, the forest's super efficient cleanup crew, remains thousands—even millions—of ants strong.

Looking Back

- Take another look at the different members of an army ant colony: the queen on page 5, the male on page 33, the minor workers on page 9, and other workers on page 6. Think of at least three different features you could use to sort the ants into two groups: those that have these features and those that don't.

- Check out the ants on page 23. Just like people, ants have joints so their hard skeleton can bend. Unlike people, the joints are easy to see because the ant skeleton is on the outside of the body. Look closely to see what an ant's joints look like. How do you think it helps an ant to have lots of joints?

- Did you notice how the ants used their hooked claws to hold onto each other on page 28? Look back through the book to see the other ants in action. Why would the hooked claws on the tips of their feet help them climb and walk?

Glossary

ANTENNAE: two movable structures on the ant's head

BROOD: the eggs and developing young

CARRION: a dead animal that a scavenger eats

COLONY: a group of ants living together

CROP: a sacklike part of an ant's digestive track where food is stored

DIGESTIVE SYSTEM: the system of organs that breaks food down for use by the body

EGG: a reproductive cell produced by the queen

LARVA (LARVAE): the life stage of an ant in which it grows

MANDIBLES: toothlike mouthparts

PHEROMONE: a chemical scent produced by ants and other animals

PREDATOR: an animal that hunts and eats other animals in order to survive

PREY: an animal that a predator catches to eat

PUPA (PUPAE): the life stage of an ant in which it changes into an adult

SCAVENGER: an animal that feeds on dead animals

SWARM: a large group of ants foraging for food

More Information

BOOKS

Holldobler, Burt, and Edward O. Wilson. *The Ants.*
Cambridge, MA: Belknap Press, 1990. For older readers,
this winner of the Pulitzer Prize for nonfiction in 1991
presents an accessible and fascinating account of the lives
of many different kinds of ants, including army ants.

Lisker, Tom. *Terror in the Tropics—Army Ants.* Austin,
TX: Steck-Vaughn Company, 1999. The author gives
information about the habits and social interactions of
army ants and how they affect people.

Sayre, April Pulley. *Army Ant Parade.* New York: Henry
Holt and Company, 2002. This book describes the sights
and sounds of being in the midst of an army ant colony
swarm as it crosses a forest floor.

VIDEO
Nova: Little Creatures Who Run the World (Nova, 1995).
Discover lots of different kinds of ants, see how they get
strength from working together, and investigate their
amazing habits.

WEBSITE
Insecta Inspecta World.
http://www.insecta-inspecta.com/ants/army/index.html
Find out more about the habits of army ants.

Index

With love for Garrett Myers and his parents Tracy and Stan

The author would like to thank the following people for sharing their expertise and enthusiasm: Dr. William H. Gotwald, Jr., emeritus professor of Biology, Utica College, Utica, New York; Dr. Michael Kaspari, Department of Zoology, University of Oklahoma, Norman, Oklahoma; and Scott Powel, School of Biological Sciences, University of Bristol, Bristol, United Kingdom. A very special thank you to Skip Jeffery for sharing the creative process and my life.

Photo Acknowledgments

The photographs in this book are used with permission of: © Alex Wild, pp. 1, 6, 7, 23, 24; © Christian Ziegler, pp. 3, 9, 12, 16, 19, 29, 31, 32, 33, 37; © Scott Powell, pp. 4, 5, 8, 11, 17, 28, 30; © Ken Preston-Mafham/Premaphotos, pp. 15, 21, 27; © William H. Gotwald, Jr., p. 35.
Front cover: © Christian Ziegler.
Back cover (top): © Scott Powell.
Back cover (bottom): *Army Ants*: © Christian Ziegler; *Hyenas*: © Richard du Toit/naturepl.com; *Jackals*: © Beverly Joubert/National Geographic/Getty Images; *Tasmanian Devils*: Photodisc Royalty Free by Getty Images; *Vultures*: © Chris Hellier/CORBIS; *Wolverines*: © Daniel J. Cox/naturalexposures.com.

Lerner Publications Company
A division of Lerner Publishing Group
241 First Avenue North
Minneapolis, MN 55401

Website address:www.lernerbooks.com

Library of Congress Cataloging-in-Publication Data

Markle, Sandra.
    Army ants / by Sandra Markle.
      p.   cm.—(Animal scavengers)
    Includes bibliographical references and index.
    ISBN-13: 978–0–8225–3196–8 (lib. bdg. : alk. paper)
    ISBN-10: 0–8225–3196–8 (lib. bdg. : alk. paper)
    1. Army ants—Juvenile literature. I. Title. II. Series: Markle, Sandra. Animal scavengers.
QL568.F7M374 2005
595.79'6—dc22   2004029668

Manufactured in the United States of America
1 2 3 4 5 6 – DP – 10 09 08 07 06 05

READ ANIMAL PREDATORS, A *BOOKLIST* TOP 10 YOUTH NONFICTION SERIES BY SANDRA MARKLE

Crocodiles
Great White Sharks
Killer Whales
Lions
Owls
Polar Bears
Wolves